Tiny Moments Of Joy

Spotted on Market Day in
Aotearoa New Zealand

Tiny Moments Of Joy

Spotted on Market Day in
Aotearoa New Zealand

George Penney

SWASHBUCKLER PRESS

First published by Swashbuckler Press Limited in 2025.
Copyright © 2025 by George Penney
All rights reserved.

Print ISBN: 978-1-0671116-0-1
Ebook ISBN: 978-1-0671116-1-8

No portion of this book may be reproduced in any form without written permission from the publisher or author, except as permitted by New Zealand copyright law.

No part of this book may be used in any manner in the learning, training or development of generative artificial intelligence technologies (including but not limited to machine learning models and large language models (LLMs)), whether by data scraping, data mining or use in any way to create or form a part of data sets or in any other way.

No written content in this book has been created with A.I.

In fact, the author would not trust A.I. to make a cup of tea. It would probably forget to warm the pot, put the milk in first and then only serve stale biscuits for dunking. We do not approve.

To my wonderful supporters and readers.
You are an endless source of delight.

Contents

Introduction	7
Summer	10
Autumn	64
Winter	122
Spring	174
Year's End	226
Afterward	245
Glossary	246
Special Thanks	250
Acknowledgements	251
About the Author	252
Also By The Author	253
Typo Disclaimer	255

Introduction

Kia ora koutou, (Hello!)

I'm so glad you could join me for a year of tiny joyful moments, spotted in everyday life here in Aotearoa New Zealand.

Feeling joy, even for a brief instant, breeds resilience. It creates room to think, to pause, to breathe. Noticing even the smallest moments of positivity around us can sometimes be a life preserver on the darkest days.

Each of the moments you're about to read are fleeting, usually observed and noted down in mere seconds as I've gone about my regular market day activities of shopping for groceries, stopping to chat to friends and enjoying a pot of tea.

They are not remarkable in that they're merely a reflection of people being themselves—as people are everywhere, every moment of the day around the globe. But nevertheless, in a world that is increasingly fraught and divided, I see noticing them as a profound act of resistance.

In 2023 I started sharing the small things I've always noticed everyday, and much to my delight, I soon learned that I'm not the only one who feels this way.

Over the past two years my wonderful readers have told me that they've read my small observations to lighten their daily commute, to get to sleep, to help them start their day, while recovering from injury, while going through chemotherapy and—in one very unique instance—to distract themselves while they were in labour!

Observing the tiny moments of joy around us is an active reminder that there is still hope in the world. It reminds us of what we have in common, rather than what divides us.

If you look around you, you'll find joy everywhere. It may be hearing someone singing to themselves in their garden as you walk down your street. It may be the goofy look your dog gives you when she sees you want to play ball. It may simply be the way steam drifts from your first coffee of the day.

In the following pages, we're going to spot people of all ages, makes and models buying groceries and delicious treats, browsing local arts and crafts and—rather more often than you may expect—showing off their best dinosaur and fairy costumes.

Following the seasons, we start with January in the

height of New Zealand's summer, then travel through to the year's end. And as you wander with me, I hope you'll find some space to relax for a little while, to put put your feet up, to breathe deeply and to smile.

Ngā mihi (Thank you)
George Penney

P.S. Please feel free to consult the glossary at the back of this book if you encounter any words you aren't familiar with.

And finally, this book has been written in New Zealand English, which means that there may be the odd additional 'l', 's' or 'u' that you're unfamiliar with. I encourage you to see these differences as a celebration of the breadth of the English language. It pays not to take these things too seriously.

Summer

Summer in New Zealand means the click-click-whir of cicadas in the trees, the smell of green on a warm breeze. It means bright blue skies and the promise of the beach on a lazy Sunday. It means tramping along (mostly) dry tracks, navigating snarled tree roots and mighty inclines that the average Kiwi describes as "easy". It means barbecues, Waitangi Day and freedom campers. It means strawberries, cherries and fresh tomatoes. It means bare feet, shorts, T-shirts and summer dresses. It means a wander to the dairy to buy an ice cream and the smell of sunscreen. It means long days and making plans to catch up later. It means small humans dressed as dinosaurs and fairies stomping around having fun.

Aotearoa smiles when the summer sun shines.

❖ ❖ ❖

A man (80s?)
ambles through the markets
seemingly oblivious to
the peristalsis-like pulses
of the crowd surrounding him.

He's wearing a vivid purple shirt,
stripy purple pants
and sparkly purple Crocs
that glimmer in the sunlight.

His hands are clasped behind his back
as he smiles to himself.

It is a good day.

❖ ❖ ❖

✦ ✦ ✦

A small human is fervently trying
to convince his dad
that he needs FOUR
sausages in a bun
to survive.

A dying swan act is implemented.
Dad is impervious.

Moments later Small Human declares he doesn't like
sausages and just wants a bun.

Then he declares that he just wants the tomato sauce.

He is later seen with his face covered in mustard.

✦ ✦ ✦

A woman is striding
through a crowd of people
while holding a bouquet
of lilies
above her head
like a battle flag.

Her expression is determined,
her pace is brisk.

Her wheelie cart has a giant bag
of cherries in it.

She's got important
fruit business
to attend to.

❖ ❖ ❖

A young sheepdog
in training has
firm opinions
about the direction
he would like to be going
and is straining
horizontally on his leash.

If he had his way,
all these disorderly humans
would be rounded up
and organised.

And the one closest to him would
DEFINITELY
give him a bite of that hot dog.

❖ ❖ ❖

❖ ❖ ❖

A married couple (80s?)
is arguing with each other
at an ATM.

They're bickering about
him being slow,
how he's always slow
and how people are watching.

Finally he bows to the people waiting, saying,
"Thank you for attending a performance
of the world's longest running drama."

He wanders off grinning
as his wife follows, laughing.

❖ ❖ ❖

❖ ❖ ❖

Two extremely optimistic tourists
are taking
over twenty minutes
to make a thirty-point-turn
in a huge camper van
on a narrow street,
right next to a bustling market.

There are many spectators
by the end
of their magnificent feat
and loud applause
sees them on their way.

❖ ❖ ❖

❖ ❖ ❖

A man (60s?)
wearing a blue singlet,
khaki work shorts
and jandals
is walking along,
practising a speech
that's been written
on a piece of notepaper
covered in scrawled cursive writing.

His expression is concerned
and he scratches his beard thoughtfully
as he mumbles
"Thank you all for comin' out today…"

❖ ❖ ❖

A small human (6?)
is walking into the markets,
tugging his dad along by the hand.

Dad asks where they're going
and Small Human announces dramatically,
"I CAN'T SURVIVE without bacon!"

Dad laughs and they head for
the Māori fried bread truck
for breakfast.

❖ ❖ ❖

A tiny human (2?)
is sitting in a stroller
with a big punnet of strawberries
on her lap.

She's cheerfully mashing them
into her mouth
with one hand
while waving at passersby
with the other.

This is the BEST thing EVER.

❖ ❖ ❖

❖ ❖ ❖

A woman (80s?)
in a bright yellow shirt
and a teen (14?)
are ambling past a chai stall.

As they walk, she hip bumps the teen.
"Tell me today's good thing about you."

Teen smiles.
"Ah. I'm good at soaking up the sun?"

She laughs
wrapping an arm around his waist.
"Sounds about right."

❖ ❖ ❖

❖ ❖ ❖

A tall man (30s?)
with full-body tattoos
wearing a Mötley Crüe T-shirt,
is dancing
with a small human (5?)
wearing a rainbow dress.

They're both getting their made-up steps wrong
and their giggles ring
up and down
the footpath.

❖ ❖ ❖

A small human (3?)
has been given a coin
to put in a busker's hat.

He spots a bunch of coins
already there
and is soon squatting
over this newfound treasure
like Smaug
lurking on his mighty hoard.

The busker starts laughing so much
she can't sing anymore
and Mum is now stepping in to
explain the idea of ownership.

Small Human is not convinced.

❖ ❖ ❖

A pensive woman (20s?)
is walking past
an organic beauty products stall.

She asks her friend,
"Do you think it's possible to have
a pot plant addiction?
Because I've got three monsteras
and I almost just bought another one."

❖ ❖ ❖

❖ ❖ ❖

Two women (40s?)
are sitting side-by-side
at a colourfully painted
public piano.

They're belting out a tune
that started as Chopsticks,
but one's sped up faster
than the other.

And now they're
howling with laughter
as the melody falls apart.

❖ ❖ ❖

❖ ❖ ❖

A tiny human (1?)
has worked out
that blowing raspberries
at strangers
is a LOT of fun.

Especially when different strangers
of all ages, makes
and models
blow raspberries
right back at her.

Delighted chortles ring through the air.

❖ ❖ ❖

❖ ❖ ❖

Two small humans (5?)
are taste-testing
different types of honey.

They're providing detailed notes
on each one's yumminess
to the vendor who is nodding
with all seriousness.

He asks which one they like best
and after much deliberation
they pick the cinnamon.

❖ ❖ ❖

❖ ❖ ❖

A small human (2?)
is given a donut
by Mum.

He decides that the appropriate way
to eat it is
by mashing
the jammy middle
into his face.

It does not quite work as planned,
but the result is pleasing anyway.

Jam all over his nose and eyelashes
Mum belly laughing
while trying to clean him up.

❖ ❖ ❖

❖ ❖ ❖

Two barefoot women (18?)
in bikinis
with towels wrapped around their waists
are walking out of a dairy
with ice creams.

It's a rainy day
but they're headed to the beach,
laughing and talking to each other
as a light drizzle mists their hair.

This is happiness.

❖ ❖ ❖

❖ ❖ ❖

At a candied nut stall

a man (60s?)

sidles up to another (50s?)

and asks out the corner of his mouth,

"So... Are you still doin' the vinyl, mate?"

with the air of someone

asking a friend

if they still have

that hydroponic weed set-up

in their garden shed.

Secret music talk ensues.

❖ ❖ ❖

✦ ✦ ✦

A small human (3?)
has suddenly lost
all use of her legs
right in front of
a Dutch pancake stand.
(Oh no!)

In between being a floppy jelly
on the ground
she sneaks optimistic looks
at the pancake production
taking place nearby.

For some strange reason
Dad isn't buying the act.

✦ ✦ ✦

❖ ❖ ❖

A young human (6?)
in sensible overalls
and pink gumboots
is walking down a shady street.

A sleek black cat is at her side
trotting along on a leash.

Both Black Cat and Young Human
seem happy with this arrangement,
including the bit
where they both pause their walk
to jump on fallen leaves.

❖ ❖ ❖

❖ ❖ ❖

A woman (70s?) is talking to
a man (70s?) in a café.

She says,
"You know that singer that sounds like a squashed frog.
The one you like?"

He replies, "Bob Dylan."

"No.
The one who sounds like a squashed frog.
He croaks."

He replies, "Bob Dylan."

She frowns. "No. He sounds like—"

He sighs. "Bob Dylan."

❖ ❖ ❖

❖ ❖ ❖

A small human (3?)
has somehow gotten a hold
of a fistful of sugar packets
and is strutting through the markets,
holding them like
a conquering knight
clutching the spoils of victory.

That is, until Mum
asks where they came from.

Small Conquering Knight
suddenly has no idea,
but insists they are rightfully hers
because she's holding them.

❖ ❖ ❖

❖ ❖ ❖

A deadpan woman (40s?)
in a green raincoat
asks a florist,
"Do you have any flowers that say,
'You shit me, but I love you anyway?'"

The florist pauses,
looks thoughtful
then nods decisively.
"Yeah. I think I can manage that."

❖ ❖ ❖

❖ ❖ ❖

A small human (4?)
is wearing
some new sparkly shoes.

She is extremely proud of them
and is doing her best
to draw attention to them
every opportunity she gets.

What ensues is a complex
and wonderful dance
that involves sticking her feet out
at every possible chance
to catch the light.

Her big brother (6?)
looks on,
incredulous.

❖ ❖ ❖

✦ ✦ ✦

A tiny human (2?)
is toddling
next to his mum
when he sees
some celery tops
poking out of someone's bag
at eye-height.

Suddenly he's on a mission.

Celery tops are the thing
he wants to touch
THE MOST
in the whole world.

Mum's saying no,
but this is celery.
This is IMPORTANT.

✦ ✦ ✦

❖ ❖ ❖

A small human (5?)
in a Batman costume
has been caught with his family
in the rain.

Mum, Dad and Sister
are looking very put out,
huddling in the lee of a building.

But Small Human Superhero
is beaming,
arms outstretched.

He is Batman!
Rain is no obstacle!
Batman is impervious to weather!

❖ ❖ ❖

❖ ❖ ❖

A man (80s?)
with an epic soup strainer moustache
is talking to a friend
at a coffee cart.

He says,
"You ever feel the need to create mayhem, mate?"

His friend shrugs.
"Sometimes. Depends."

Mayhem Man grins.
"That's how I feel now."

He stirs four sugars into his cappuccino.

❖ ❖ ❖

❖ ❖ ❖

Two women (30s?)
are stealing a smooch
behind a bakery truck.

It's pouring with rain
but they're snuggled together
under an umbrella.

Bags of vegetables at their feet
are getting wet
but they don't care.

A tiny perfect moment.

❖ ❖ ❖

❖ ❖ ❖

A man (30s?)
has just bought four bars
of handmade soap
before realising that
he doesn't have a bag.

The pockets of his cargo shorts
provide the perfect solution
and he pops them in
before stepping out into pouring rain.

He's seen ruefully answering
a friend's questions
about his sudsy shorts
a short time later.

❖ ❖ ❖

❖ ❖ ❖

A woman (70s?)
sidles up to
a fruit and vegetable vendor
with theatrical nonchalance.
"So… Do you have any of those
special tomatoes for me?"

Nodding, expression enigmatic,
he pulls a box of
heirloom tomatoes
out from under his table.

They share a conspiratorial grin.

❖ ❖ ❖

❖ ❖ ❖

A small human (4?)
is fidgeting on the spot
as her mum
buys a box of strawberries.

Small Human does not seem
impressed by strawberries.
There is something much bigger
on her mind.

Suddenly she bellows,
"MY NANA CALLS ME HER LITTLE BLUEBERRY!"

She looks expectantly around her
for people to be suitably impressed.
(They are.)

❖ ❖ ❖

❖ ❖ ❖

Two small humans (3?)
spot each other in a crowd.

One's wearing a Spider-Man suit.
One's wearing bright blue overalls.

They run towards each other
and meet in a hug
that knocks Spider-Man over.

No one seems to mind
and they're soon
chattering enthusiastically.

❖ ❖ ❖

❖ ❖ ❖

A small human (5?)
in a green flowery dress
is getting exasperated
that her sparkly handbag
has a strap that's too long.

Dad offers to wear it for her
and is soon seen
wandering through the markets
rocking sparkly fashion
over the top of his All Blacks jersey
like a seasoned diva.

❖ ❖ ❖

A tiny human (2?)
spots a fire truck passing
and he excitedly shouts,
"Fire truck!"

Not satisfied that people have grasped
the awesomeness of this situation
he runs around
the nearby market goers
telling each of them
about the fire truck,
his earnest expression conveying
just how important this news is.

❖ ❖ ❖

At a stall selling

jumpers, beanies and gloves

made of homespun wool,

a woman (50s?)

is chilling in a camp chair,

knitting while chatting to friends

who come and go.

A small human (4?)

approaches and asks,

"How do you DO that?"

and a demonstration is soon underway.

A new crafter is in the making!

❖ ❖ ❖

❖ ❖ ❖

A young human (9?)
is inspecting a basil plant,
her face a map of concentration.

She asks her dad,
"Do you think this one will like our house?"

He wraps an arm around her shoulders.
"Yeah. I think it'll be alright.
Want to get it a buddy?"

❖ ❖ ❖

❖ ❖ ❖

At a fruit and vegetable stall
a small human (3?)
is helping Mum pick nectarines.

Although,
she is somewhat indignant
that Mum doesn't appreciate her method
of biting into each one
to make sure they're just right.

She's a fruit connoisseur
who is being stifled
in her quest for perfection!

❖ ❖ ❖

❖ ❖ ❖

A woman (20s?)
selects
five jewel-green zucchinis
at an organic vegetable stall.

She departs with a spring in her step,
holding them lovingly to her chest
as she crosses
to an artisanal cheese stall.

Hunting and gathering deliciousness.

❖ ❖ ❖

❖ ❖ ❖

A man (60s?)
sits on a curb
while lovingly polishing his
vintage Royal Enfield motorbike.
Led Zeppelin's *Immigrant Song*
is playing on the cassette deck
at his hip
and his expression
is verging on zen.

Cicadas clicking in the trees
all around,
a 1920s cottage in the background.

❖ ❖ ❖

❖ ❖ ❖

A small human (4?)
is frowning with fierce intensity
at his big brother (6?)
who's eating a hot dog, bun first.

Finally, when he can't take it anymore,
he bellows,
"YOU'RE DOING IT WRONG!
You have to eat the
SAUSAGE BIT FIRST!"

Big Brother goes on munching.
He cares not for the Sausage Police.

❖ ❖ ❖

❖ ❖ ❖

A man (30s?)
wearing a bucket hat and boardshorts,
finishes up a conversation
with another man (20s?).

Slapping him heartily on the shoulder he says,
"Call me if you're havin' a rough one, yeah?
Day or night."

He waits until his friend nods
and then heads off
to spread the awesomeness
elsewhere.

❖ ❖ ❖

❖ ❖ ❖

Two women (50s?)
are lounging in rattan chairs
on the footpath
in front of a small gallery
that opens
whenever the artist feels like it.

They're enjoying a sunbeam,
chatting about life and the weather.

A pot of tea and two cups
sitting between them.

A big fluffy cat wandering over
for smooches.

❖ ❖ ❖

❖ ❖ ❖

On Waitangi Day:
A tiny human (2?)
is being carried
around the wharenui of a marae
by his dad (20s?)
who's showing him
the carvings and is describing
what they mean.

Dad beaming with pride.
Tiny Human beaming at Dad.

❖ ❖ ❖

❖ ❖ ❖

On Waitangi Day:
Three men (30s?)
are kicking back on some grass,
big plates of food by their side,
shoes off,
vibe totally chill.

As a big group passes by
they call out,
"Happy Waitangi Day whānau!"

People stop by
for a chat and to ask
which food trucks they've tried.

❖ ❖ ❖

A French Bulldog
is being held in the arms
of his human
who is ordering a bacon roll.

French Bulldog's eyes are wild
with excitement,
his nose twitching
at super-sonic speed.

The air is delicious
and he wants to eat ALL of it.

❖ ❖ ❖

A small human (3?)
has just been given
a strawberry ice cream cone
by Dad.

Small Human does a small dance,
only to trip and fall forward,
mashing the lot
into the front of Dad's shorts.

Perfect bullseye.

Dad sighing.
Mum cry-laughing.
Small Human wanting more ice cream.

❖ ❖ ❖

❖ ❖ ❖

A small human (3?)
is strutting next to his dad.

His hands are
stretched out in front of him
like he's holding a steering wheel,
his gaze is focused
and he's making mighty
BRUM BRUM
noises.

He's the driver of an invisible
but impressive big rig
and he's navigating it
around this market
like a seasoned professional.

❖ ❖ ❖

❖ ❖ ❖

A man (20s?)

is sitting

near a bakery truck.

He's holding a box of vegetables

and is smiling dreamily

as he looks through

his magnificent purchases.

Fresh cherry tomatoes,

cucumbers

and a big punnet of strawberries

peek out the top.

❖ ❖ ❖

❖ ❖ ❖

A woman (60s?)
in sensible hiking gear
is walking behind a man (60s?)
who's laughing
and telling her she's horrible.

As she's walking,
she's covertly poking him on the bottom
with a new wooden spoon,
her mouth curved in a faint
but cheeky
smile.

❖ ❖ ❖

❖ ❖ ❖

A woman (80s?)
in green overalls,
parks her walker
in front of a cherry stall.

Grinning at the stall owner
she points to the basket in the front
and says,
"Load me up buttercup!"

Laughing,
the vendor picks out a box of cherries
and stows them for her.

❖ ❖ ❖

❖ ❖ ❖

A woman (60s?)
is walking with a small human (4?)
who is holding up a sprig of kōwhai
in front of her face.

Small Human is in stealth mode.

Meanwhile Gran is saying,
"Gran's getting a coffee first
and then we'll come up with a plan of action.
Sound good?"

Small Human's leaves rustle in approval.

❖ ❖ ❖

Autumn

Autumn in New Zealand is show-off trees turning orange and red on the hills and mountains.

It's colourful leaves falling on footpaths. It's cicadas still going strong, at least for a little bit. It's feijoas everywhere. It's Fringe time with creative people from all over the world touring through the country.

It's cooler nights and getting the warmer clothes down from the top shelf of the wardrobe. It's walking optimistically by the cheese truck to see if raclette is on the menu again.

It's buying the last of the summer tomatoes, knowing they won't be seen this cheap again for months. It's watching the weather forecast for rain and snow.

Aotearoa in the Autumn is beautiful.

❖ ❖ ❖

A man (30s?)
approaches a cheese stand
and declares
that he would like to buy
the stinkiest cheese they have available.

A delightful conversation follows
about how to measure
cheese stinkiness vs deliciousness.

A suitably stinky cheese is located.
All parties seem content.

❖ ❖ ❖

❖ ❖ ❖

A woman (30s?)
takes an epic dive to intercept
her small human's scoop of ice cream
as it falls off the cone.

She catches it in her hand
with a look of absolute triumph.

Small Human remains oblivious.

❖ ❖ ❖

❖ ❖ ❖

A woman with a tiny dog
is telling a mushroom vendor
that she can't buy oyster mushrooms
because her tiny dog is terrified of them.

Meanwhile,
Tiny Dog is at her feet,
making sure his own personal mushrooms
are perfectly polished.

❖ ❖ ❖

❖ ❖ ❖

A tourist samples
all the petit fours
at a French pâtisserie stall
before deciding to buy two of each.

When the vendor asks if they're a gift,
she replies,
"It's lunch!"
with a gleeful cackle.

❖ ❖ ❖

❖ ❖ ❖

A couple (50s?)
are buying avocados.
One selects three
after careful and slow consideration
—sniffing, juggling, long staring—
only for their partner to stealthily put them back
and select another three
with the vibe of someone
carrying out a diamond heist.

❖ ❖ ❖

❖ ❖ ❖

A man (80s?)
orders a cappuccino from a coffee cart
only to grumpily announce
that they're trying to poison him
and that he'll need urgent medical intervention
or he'll die.

The barista
—obviously an old friend—
offers to make him another coffee for free
to hurry the process.

❖ ❖ ❖

A tiny white dog
is desperately trying
to convince his humans
that he deserves some of their cake
by means of some
INTENSE
staring and mind control.

No noise, just staring.
Intense, intense staring.

Cake achieved.

❖ ❖ ❖

A woman (20s?)
is buying a plain baguette
from an artisanal bakery stall.

She sniffs it,
grins and bites off a big chunk.
She then walks off,
chewing happily.

❖ ❖ ❖

❖ ❖ ❖

A golden retriever
has been temporarily tethered
near a whitebait and seafood truck
and is plaintively
"awooing" and "uffing"
to anyone nearby,
telling them of his great
trials and tribulations
in being deprived
of such tantalizing deliciousness.

❖ ❖ ❖

❖ ❖ ❖

A man (40s?)
is walking along
with a plunger stuck to his bald head.

An accompanying teen (14?)
is dying of dad-based embarrassment
that intensifies
when Dad starts nodding his head,
causing the plunger to waggle.

Her younger sibling is highly amused
at both Dad's antics
and Big Sister's mortification.

❖ ❖ ❖

✦ ✦ ✦

A woman (50s?)
enthusiastically greets another
and asks how she is.

The other gives her a big hug
and announces that her macadamia tree
is going to fruit this year.

Excitement all round.

✦ ✦ ✦

❖ ❖ ❖

A man resembling an anxious wizard
is talking to a friend
near a granola stall.

He says,
"I don't think I'm emotionally ready
for macadamia nuts."

His friend nods in understanding
and the conversation moves on.

❖ ❖ ❖

❖ ❖ ❖

A man (60s?)

says,

"I think I'll get a cheese scone,"

and veers towards a cheese truck.

The woman accompanying him (60s?)

speaks with sort of tone used

to address a puppy next to a suspicious puddle.

"You don't like cheese scones."

The man veers away from the cheese truck.

❖ ❖ ❖

❖ ❖ ❖

Two men in plaid shirts,
sturdy shorts and work boots,
are standing next to a woolly hat display.

One says to the other,
"Did you hear about Jane?
She got TWO sheds."

There's a pause, then the other replies,
"Two sheds?"

"Yeah. Two."

Second guy shakes his head,
"Yeah. Wow. Two sheds."

Contemplative silence follows.

❖ ❖ ❖

❖ ❖ ❖

A teen (13?)
asks his mum,
"How much are you worth?"
after explaining it's important
to know for jobs in the future.

Mum laughs and says,
"I'm priceless."

Teen comes straight back with,
"No, you're depreciating!"

❖ ❖ ❖

❖ ❖ ❖

A man (80s?)
wearing a homburg and a cardigan,
is dancing on his own
next to a busker who is playing jazz
on the piano.

His expression is
one hundred percent content.

❖ ❖ ❖

❖ ❖ ❖

A small human (3?)
is asked to hold Mum's hand.

He shouts,
"No!"
and stomps off
to grab on to the hand
of a passing tourist
who finds the whole thing hilarious.

Passing Tourist says to Mum
that she'll keep him
as long as he likes broccoli.

Small Human shouts,
"No!"
and marches back to Mum.

❖ ❖ ❖

❖ ❖ ❖

A small human (4?)
inspects avocados
before roaring at the stall owner,
"DO BEES LIKE AVOCADOS?"

The stall owner answers in the affirmative
that bees do indeed like avocado trees.

Intrepid Junior Bee Scientist
looks sceptical and long suffering.
"But do they like AVOCADOS?!"

❖ ❖ ❖

❖ ❖ ❖

A man (60s?)

on a pushbike

is riding down a hill

behind a woman of around the same age.

He yells out,

"I love you!"

She yells back,

"What?"

He yells back,

"I love you, stupid."

She yells back, laughing,

"I know.

You don't have to be rude about it.

Idiot."

They cycle on.

❖ ❖ ❖

At a fruit and vegetable stall,
a man (40s?)
buys a leek
and brandishes it at his teen son,
saying,
"En garde!"

Teen Son parries with the head of broccoli
they've just purchased
and soon they're jousting
back and forward.

Food fighting at its most sophisticated.
Vege soup for dinner tonight!

❖ ❖ ❖

A man (20s?)

is swiftly walking through the markets

with a cloth shopping bag

tightly packed

with at least four large bunches of celery.

He's grinning to himself

like he has

secret exciting

celery business to attend to.

❖ ❖ ❖

❖ ❖ ❖

Two young humans (7?)
are peering at the plants
at a carnivorous plant stall.

One looks at the other speculatively
and says,
"Do you think they eat people?"

The other says confidently,
"Probably not, like, well...
maybe your finger if you let it."

❖ ❖ ❖

❖ ❖ ❖

A small human (5?)
in a red corduroy dress,
is doing an improvised interpretive dance
next to her mum.

People are chatting,
laughing and flowing around her,
but she doesn't mind.

After a very impressive pirouette,
she finishes,
does a short bow
and looks around expectantly.

A nearby couple (50s?)
applauds.

❖ ❖ ❖

❖ ❖ ❖

A backpacker (20s?)
with a heavy pack
that has a ukulele strapped to it,
is watching a jazz pianist
knocking out an epic riff.

Backpacker is having a fantastic time
and is wearing a huge grin,
his hands slapping on his thighs.

A holiday experience to remember for later.

❖ ❖ ❖

✦ ✦ ✦

A man (20s?)
walks up to a coffee cart
and notices that there's a big queue.

He frowns,
stretches his neck from side to side
and gives his body a loosen-up shake
before stepping into line.

Queuing is tough business,
but he's now prepared.

The coffee is worth it.

✦ ✦ ✦

A small human (3?)
in tiny work boots, shorts
and a John Deere T-shirt,
is holding a pot of parsley.

Looking appraisingly at the parsley,
he says,
"I can cook LOTS of things with this,
can't I Mum?
I can cook more than anyone else in the
WHOLE WORLD."

❖ ❖ ❖

A tiny new human is sitting
in a shark-patterned baby carrier.

She's all huge eyes
as she inspects her surroundings,
giving the world a gummy grin
when she spots someone walking by
with a bright green scarf.

Everything is exciting.
Everything is colours!

❖ ❖ ❖

❖ ❖ ❖

A tiny human (2?)
is astraddle a push-along tricycle,
staring ahead
with race-car-driver intensity.

Nan's pushing,
and every now and then
he bellows the command,
"TURNING!"

Nan cheerfully makes
click-clack indicator noises
while Tiny Race Car Driver
leans into the corners.

❖ ❖ ❖

✦ ✦ ✦

A young human (10?)
wearing a bucket hat,
is helping his dad sell
grapes fresh-picked from their family vineyard.

Whenever anyone pays,
he very seriously gives them
a double thumbs up,
full eye contact.

An adorable salesman saying thank you.
(His dad looking on with a bemused smile.)

✦ ✦ ✦

❖ ❖ ❖

A man (60s?)
tries a fresh fig
at a friend's fruit stall
and says,
"Ya don't need blue pills if you eat one of these,
I tell ya."

His wife snort-laughs, retorting,
"Well THAT came outa left field!"

❖ ❖ ❖

❖ ❖ ❖

A small human (6?)
in a T-shirt with tractors on it,
is stomping next to his dad.

He says indignantly,
"I just asked if I could try Dad. I asked!"

Dad stifles a laugh,
"Yeah, ya did matey.
But when you ask to try a cheese sample,
you don't keep going back
until there's none left."

❖ ❖ ❖

❖ ❖ ❖

A small human (5?)
in fluffy red shoes
is snaffling strawberries
from her mum's shopping basket.

But instead of eating them,
Small Human is stuffing them in her cheeks
like a sneaky strawberry squirrel.

Nothing to see here.
Nope!
Nothing. At. All.

❖ ❖ ❖

✦ ✦ ✦

A small human (3?)

has just raced

out of the shower and laundry block

at the centre of the markets

and is doing a nudie run

with Dad in hot pursuit!

Small Human is told

he's gotta get dressed

at their campervan before lunch,

but he's having none of it.

Who needs clothes on a sunny day like this?!

✦ ✦ ✦

❖ ❖ ❖

A man (60s?)
brings two coffees
over to a table
where his friend is waiting.

With a conspiratorial grin he says,
"I've just thought of
the PERFECT gift for Rose, mate.
You can't go wrong.
What you've gotta do
is buy her a chess set!
You can never go wrong with a chess set!"

❖ ❖ ❖

❖ ❖ ❖

A man (70s?)
is sitting
companionably with his Schnauzer
at a Dutch poffertjes stall.

One tiny pancake for human,
one for dog friend.

Finally they're finished.

He stands up and says,
"We're just going for a walk
around the market, Harry,
if that's alright with you."

Harry the Dog gives him a tail wag
and then they're on their way.

❖ ❖ ❖

❖ ❖ ❖

A young human (7?)
is talking to a friend.

He says,
"Do you know satay?
It's cool.
I ate that.
And do you... do you know uhm... yeah.
I forgot what the name was.
But that was cool too
and I ate that."

His friend seems quite intrigued.

❖ ❖ ❖

❖ ❖ ❖

At a Multicultural Festival:
A small human (3?)
wearing a pretty traditional costume,
has rolled up her sash
and has stuck it up her nose.

This is a VERY impressive trick.

Soon there's a row of small humans
with elaborate nose plugs,
wondering why their parents
aren't as impressed as they are.

❖ ❖ ❖

❖ ❖ ❖

A small human (5?)
has discovered a display
of preserved and framed beetles.

This is amazing and
Junior Bug Scientist
has many beetle facts to share.

Most of them are about
who they can beat in a fight,
but his enthusiasm is admirable
and Grandad lets him pick his favourite
to take home.

❖ ❖ ❖

❖ ❖ ❖

A man (20s?)
with an impeccably groomed
Gomez Addams moustache,
is trying on thick silver bangles
at a jewellery stall.

The owner asks if he needs help
and he earnestly says,
"I'm looking for something
that makes me look wise.
And maybe handsome."

❖ ❖ ❖

A small human (4?)
wearing a Thomas the Tank Engine hat,
is sitting on a hay bale,
admiring his strawberry ice cream.

Mum suggests he should eat it before it melts
and he gives her an offended look.
"Not yet! I want to LOOK at it first!"

❖ ❖ ❖

A small human (5?)
and her mum
are waiting in line at a food truck.

She says,
"Mum, can I have a hug?
The one you gave me earlier wasn't big enough."

Mum picks her up
for a monkey grip hug,
smiling into Small Human's hair.

❖ ❖ ❖

❖ ❖ ❖

A tiny human (1?)
is being held aloft by Dad.

But wait!

He's not a tiny human at all!
He's an aeroplane!

Zooming through the air.
Strafing Mum!
Strafing Big Sister!

Gleeful chortles accompanying
deft aeronautical feats!

❖ ❖ ❖

❖ ❖ ❖

A man (30s?)
in a death metal band T-shirt,
wearing noise cancelling headphones,
is grooving his way through the markets.

He buys a bag of tomatoes
and does a shoulder shimmy.

He reaches the end of the row
and does a spin on one foot.

He waits in line at a coffee cart
and does a quick one-two shuffle.

He's the happiest
Spectre of Darkness
in town.

❖ ❖ ❖

✦ ✦ ✦

A burly bald man (60s?)
is sitting at his stall
with a tiny new human laying on his lap.

With a huge grin he says,
"Where's a smile for Poppa?
Where's that smile?!"

Suddenly he lets out a booming,
delighted laugh.

Poppa got his smile.

✦ ✦ ✦

❖ ❖ ❖

Two small human friends (6?)
are standing at a stall selling cushions,
discussing which ones they like the best.

Junior Interior Decorators
have some very firm opinions
on the colour blue.
They feel that there should be a lot more of it.

And maybe more cushions
with space and planets on them.

The stall owner nods
with an admirably straight face
as she takes note.

This is vital cushion advice.

❖ ❖ ❖

❖ ❖ ❖

A small human (4?)
is carefully counting the money
in a small cross-stitch-decorated change purse.
She says,
"Mum! I've got FIVE HUNDRED DOLLARS!"

Her mum laughs.
"Are you sure you don't mean five dollars?"

Newly Minted Rich Small Human
looks offended.

This kind of fiscal questioning is not acceptable
when she has money to spend!

❖ ❖ ❖

❖ ❖ ❖

A high wind threatens to blow
a fruit and vegetable stall owner's awning away.

A man who's just purchased some onions
asks if she needs help
and patiently takes over holding
the awning down for her.

He's still on the job ten minutes later,
but now he's sipping a takeaway coffee
and is cheerfully chatting
with other customers.

❖ ❖ ❖

❖ ❖ ❖

A tall, sturdy man (50s?)
in a plaid shirt,
is walking through the markets,
holding a single purple cauliflower
up in the air
like it's a priceless artifact
to be admired and worshipped.

Meanwhile,
his partner gives him
a bemused look, saying,
"Seriously?"

He grins and says,
"Yup."

❖ ❖ ❖

❖ ❖ ❖

A small human (5?)
is walking slowly next to his dad,
carefully cupping
a piece of rainbow cake
in his hand
like it's a precious,
tiny bird.

He shall protect this cake at all costs.
He is the cake guardian.

❖ ❖ ❖

❖ ❖ ❖

A young human (8?)
is strutting through the markets
cradling a grow-bag for mushrooms.

His swagger is endearingly zealous.

He is the mushroom king.
He will grow them all!

❖ ❖ ❖

A woman (20s?)
minding a soap stall,
is crocheting a baby blanket.

She gets stuck on how to do a stitch
and soon three different customers
are offering to help.

All three stepping behind her table,
cheerfully giving advice
and comparing stories of times
they got stuck too.

❖ ❖ ❖

A man (50s?)
dressed in a plaid shirt, shorts,
work boots
and a battered baseball cap
is walking with a friend.

He says,
"Ya can't go wrong with quiche, mate.
Just bung a couple of eggs in a bowl.
Bit of milk.
Whack in the other stuff,
and some cheese,
and Bob's your uncle.
Quiche!
It's a bloody winner every time!"

❖ ❖ ❖

A small human (5?)
is standing sentinel
by a stall selling flowers
while his dad buys a bouquet.

Small Human is gripping
a hot dog in each hand,
his expression resolute.

He is the sausage sentinel
and will NOT
neglect his duties.

❖ ❖ ❖

A man (70s?)
in a plaid shirt,
worn jeans and work boots
is talking to a friend from around
a toothpick in the corner of his mouth.

He says,
"There are some days where all you need in life
is a bit of bread with jam on it.
It's the simple things.
Just bread. And jam."

❖ ❖ ❖

❖ ❖ ❖

A hefty Labrador
is tugging his human
towards a stall selling apples.

His human is resisting,
but Big Dog is determined!

He SHALL
inspect these apples
and he WILL
inspect them thoroughly.

Each bag gets a considered sniff
before he decides they can move on.

❖ ❖ ❖

❖ ❖ ❖

A tiny human (2?)
wearing a bunny rabbit jumper,
is keenly inspecting a display of vegetables.

Before Mum can react,
she snatches up a head of broccoli
and mashes it against her mouth.

Oh no!
This doesn't taste exactly how she'd hoped.

The disappointment is real.

Tongue poking out,
eyes screwed shut.

Nearby shoppers laughing.

❖ ❖ ❖

Winter

Winter in New Zealand is misty mornings and wet moss on bare trees. It's dark nights and talk of going to the movies. It's looking forward to Matariki. It's woolly hats and warm jumpers. It's looking to the mountains for snow fall. It's the smell of wood smoke. It's the tree in our front yard being bare of leaves so we can finally see the tūī that sits there to sing. It's silverbeet and Brussels sprouts and the kind of crisp, delicious apples I've only ever tasted here. It's getting a chilli hot chocolate at the Korean pâtisserie stall. It's standing next to each other, sharing a big bowl of tummy hugging gnocchi and bolognese from the gnocchi truck. It's meeting friends while walking into town. Stamping your feet in the cold while you chat.

Winter in Aotearoa is cosy.

A small human (3?)
stands in front of a Māori fried bread truck.
His dad asks what he wants
and he yells,
"BACON."

His dad suggests maybe
he could have something different
and he shakes his head vehemently, roaring
"BACON BACON BACON."

❖ ❖ ❖

A woman (30s?)
in kickass steampunk wear,
is complimented by a stall owner.

Just as Steampunk Woman beams, saying,
"Thank you,"
her very earnest son (6?)
replies,
"Mum says the pants ride up her bum
and give her a wedgie."

❖ ❖ ❖

❖ ❖ ❖

A Chihuahua is nested
in the arms of a woman
who's sitting at an outdoor cafe table.

Tiny Dog is snarling
like a rabid wolverine
at a passing staffy
who's inspecting a nearby tree
for widdling potential.

Staffy is not bothered.

Tiny Dog seems inconsolably furious
at this lack of respect.

❖ ❖ ❖

❖ ❖ ❖

A couple (60s?)
are having a coffee.

She's talking animatedly.
He's staring into space.

She says, "John? John? John?! JOHN?!"

He blinks. "What?"

"Are you listening?"

He looks mildly offended. "Yeah."

"Then what did I say?"

"John."

❖ ❖ ❖

A seagull is marching back and forward
in front of a man who's sitting on a bench,
eating a sausage in a bun.

Sausage Man explains to the seagull
that it's not gonna get lucky.

Persistent Seagull continues to patrol.
Sausage Man gives in and throws it a bit of his bun.

Ten other seagulls appear out of nowhere.
Chaos ensues.

❖ ❖ ❖

An endearingly grave tiny human (2?)
is lifted up by Dad
so that he can high five his uncle.

Uncle says,
"Good job my bro. You're a big boy now eh?"

Tiny Human's expression transforms
into a radiant, toothy grin.
He IS a big boy!

❖ ❖ ❖

At Matariki:

A small human runs up to his nan (80s?)
who's wearing a woven straw hat,
colourful scarves and a bright red coat.

He hugs her around the waist
and refuses to let go
when Dad asks if he wants to go
play with his cousins.

Nan picks him up
and is seen still hugging him
while he sleeps an hour later.

At Matariki:
An electrifying kapa haka performance ends
on the stage of a packed stadium
and suddenly a group of teens
in the audience stand
to do a haka back.

Then another group,
then another.

Their voices ringing to the roof,
expressions fierce.

Loud applause.
A perfect moment.

❖ ❖ ❖

A teen (14?)
dressed in a hoodie and tracksuit pants,
is holding a head of broccoli
like it's a bunch of flowers.

He offers the broccoli bouquet to his mum,
saying,
"Happy birthday".

She clutches her chest in mock surprise
before breaking into laughter.

❖ ❖ ❖

❖ ❖ ❖

Two small humans (3 & 5?)
are crouched in front of a cheese truck.

The oldest is snaffling samples for her sister.

Shoving as much cheese as possible
into their mouths
in the time it takes for Mum
to be distracted while ordering.

The vibe is unmitigated, sneaky glee.

❖ ❖ ❖

❖ ❖ ❖

A small human is objecting
most dramatically
to her bun containing a sausage,
only to go full dying swan
when her dad removes the sausage
and eats it.

Dad looks unrepentant.

Small Human punches her brother
to make herself feel better.

Brother goes full dying swan.

❖ ❖ ❖

❖ ❖ ❖

A small human (3?)
with his face and hands covered
in chocolate ice cream
is being told by his mum,
"Fin, keep your hands to yourself."

He spreads his fingers as wide as possible,
grins cheekily and roars,
"NO!"

❖ ❖ ❖

❖ ❖ ❖

A man with bare feet (20s?)
and a British accent
is talking to a stall owner.

He says,
"I came here six months ago.
I only meant to stay for two weeks
but I can't bring myself to leave yet."

Stall Owner nods in sympathy.

❖ ❖ ❖

❖ ❖ ❖

The owner of a pottery stall is explaining
to a woman (80s?)
with arthritically bent hands
that he makes sure his cups have handles
that anyone can hold.

She makes a delighted noise
when he shows her a cup
that she can grip easily.

❖ ❖ ❖

❖ ❖ ❖

A macaron vendor is explaining
to three serious small humans (5 to 8?)
how he makes his macarons.

He says,
"The trick is,
don't sift the almond meal.
They all tell ya to do it,
but don't believe them!"

All three small humans nod solemnly.

❖ ❖ ❖

❖ ❖ ❖

A very dapper man (80s?)
with a flowing white mane of hair,
a bright green coat,
blue scarf,
pressed jeans
and polished black patent leather shoes
is walking along in the sunshine,
whistling cheerfully.

He has a wrapped baguette under one arm
and a newspaper under the other.

❖ ❖ ❖

❖ ❖ ❖

A man (20?)
wearing shorts, a wool jumper
and work boots,
is talking to the owner of a stall
selling wooden bowls.

He says,
"Wow, that's a NICE bit of wood!
What sort of lathe have you got?"

Enthusiastic lathe chat ensues.

❖ ❖ ❖

❖ ❖ ❖

A small human (4?)
walking, holding his dad's hand
is asking,
"Dad, are we getting ice cream?"
"Dad, do you want some ice cream?"
"Dad, do you think they'll run out of ice cream?"

Dad is completely mellow
and repeatedly answers that ice cream is coming
once they find Mum.

Small Human looks doubtful.

❖ ❖ ❖

❖ ❖ ❖

A man (60s?)
is teaching a small human
how to play chess.

Small Human is in turn repeating everything
to her teddy which is sitting on their table.

Small Human asks Grandad,
"Do the king and queen love each other?"

❖ ❖ ❖

❖ ❖ ❖

A slender man (50s?)
with a Mephistophelean beard,
a 70s floral curtain fabric waistcoat,
a pink hat
and a Dennis the Menace T-shirt
is strutting past a fruit and vegetable stall.

He's blasting reggae music
from his shopping tote.

The strut has Prince level attitude
and is magnificent.

❖ ❖ ❖

✦ ✦ ✦

A man (40s?)
is taking a pie out of a paper bag
as he walks his basset hound.

Basset Hound flops on the ground,
making woeful wooOO noises.

Man tries tugging the lead
but Flop Dog refuses to move.

Man offers Flop Dog a bit of pie
and there's a miraculous recovery!

The Great Pie Distress is averted.

✦ ✦ ✦

❖ ❖ ❖

A small human (3?)
watches Morris Dancers perform
with a very stern frown.

He then asks his mum,
"Are they lesbians too?"

His mum laughs and says,
"Some of them might be."

He nods as if this is right and correct.

❖ ❖ ❖

❖ ❖ ❖

A small human (5?)
is walking
while hugging her Paddington Bear.

She tells Paddington that if he's good,
they'll get waffles,
before giving her mum a hopeful look.

❖ ❖ ❖

❖ ❖ ❖

A woman (20s?)

is looking at a plant stall with a friend.

She says,
"I only like the ones that don't die.
But they all die.
I try not to take it personally."

❖ ❖ ❖

❖ ❖ ❖

A man (80s?)

resembling a cheerful tortoise in a cardigan,

is saying to another man,

"So I told them

that if they wanted to come at me,

I would probably get very hurt.

But so would they!"

He brandishes his walking stick and grins.

❖ ❖ ❖

✦ ✦ ✦

A small human (3?)
is supervising his dad
as he mulches their garden.

Small Human is given a bucket
with some mulch in it
and proceeds to explain to Dad
how he is going to spread it correctly.

Dad listens, nodding in approval.

✦ ✦ ✦

❖ ❖ ❖

A small human (3?)
is eyeing off a box of daffodil badges
for Daffodil Day.

Suddenly, she grabs a handful
and runs back to her dad, shouting,
"FLOWERS!"

Her dad then makes an
unexpectedly generous
charity donation to a volunteer
who is laughing.

Small Human is later seen
with her dress covered in daffodil badges,
beaming.

❖ ❖ ❖

❖ ❖ ❖

A small human (5?)
in gumboots, jeans
and a hand-knitted green jumper
is waiting at a coffee cart,
his expression intensely focused
as he supervises the heavily tattooed barista
who is making him a fluffy.

When it's ready,
he gives it a sip
and nods
with the air of a connoisseur,
saying,
"It's very good. Thank you."

Grinning,
the barista gives him a short bow.

❖ ❖ ❖

✦ ✦ ✦

A teen (14?)
is coasting through town
on a battered BMX bike.

He's covered from helmeted head
to sneakered toes
in a thick coating of mud splatter.

A huge grin on his face.
It's been a truly excellent morning.

✦ ✦ ✦

❖ ❖ ❖

Two women (50s?)
are faux-sword fighting
with baguettes
while waiting for a friend
to order from a coffee cart.

Their friend turns
and rolls her eyes at them.

They both raspberry her in return.

❖ ❖ ❖

❖ ❖ ❖

A small, solemn human (4?)
is sitting on the display table
at his dad's fruit and vegetable stall.

He's an expert cabbage picker
and has many opinions
about the ones people should select.

Accepting all thanks as his due
with a barely perceptible nod.

Vegetables are a serious business
and one mustn't be frivolous
in their presence.

❖ ❖ ❖

❖ ❖ ❖

A small human (3?)
is sitting at a cafe table,
giving a drawing demonstration
to her very round zebra plushie.

But what is this?!

Zebra is not paying attention?!
Well, she'll see about that.

Soon Zebra is getting a stern lecture
about how to listen properly
while Mum and Nana watch on
with bemused smiles.

❖ ❖ ❖

❖ ❖ ❖

A man (20s?)
is listening
to his partner tell him
about a book
she's currently reading.

As she's talking,
he pours her a cup of tea
from the pot between them,
adding milk,
a sugar
and then waiting
with a soft, expectant smile
while she takes a sip
in between sentences.

❖ ❖ ❖

A woman (50s?)
in Victorian steampunk regalia
is talking to a curious passerby.

Resting a hand on her cogwork cane,
she says,
"We've got so many marvellous people
in our group!
All ages.
One of our members is eighty two
and she doesn't leave the house
unless she's dressed in full kit!
It's wonderful!"

A small human (3?)
has just been told that he can have
a sausage in a bun for lunch.

This is VERY exciting news
and it immediately triggers
a spectacular sausage dance
that involves many noodly moves
in addition to the word
"SAUSAGE!"
roared at random intervals.

He is the Disco Sausage King!

❖ ❖ ❖

A small human (4?)
in a crocodile onesie
is stalking through the markets.

Her steps are deliberate,
her expression is fierce
and her growls are super scary.

Although...
What is this?

A teddy bear hugged to her chest?
Ah.
Maybe even crocodiles
need something to cuddle sometimes.

❖ ❖ ❖

❖ ❖ ❖

A very big and fluffy cat
is holding court on a street corner,
greeting a steady stream of people
walking into town.

People of all ages,
makes and models
pause to give him a scootch around the ears
and to admire
his purring magnificence.

❖ ❖ ❖

❖ ❖ ❖

A tiny human (2?)
is toddling after a seagull
while roaring,
"SHOO SHOO SHOO!"

The seagull does not seem
too bothered by this
and is now walking in circles.

Tiny Human Bird Deterrent
follows,
only to soon be very dizzy!

She sits down
and frowns
at the seagull instead.

Yes.
Maybe this works much better.

❖ ❖ ❖

✦ ✦ ✦

At a bespoke knife stall,
two young humans (7 & 9?)
are peppering a bladesmith with questions
about how he gets his knives so sharp.

They're given a thorough explanation
that matches the solemnity of their enquiries.

Caring for one's tools is serious business.

✦ ✦ ✦

❖ ❖ ❖

A man (30s?)
leaves a boutique chocolate stall
with three bars
only for his partner to ask
what types he got.

He glances down at the labels
and looks up in alarm.
"I've made a tactical chocolate error
and picked the wrong ones!"

She laughs,
"Well then.
You'll just have to go get some more,
won't you?!"

They decide that this is
an excellent solution.

❖ ❖ ❖

❖ ❖ ❖

A man (60s?)
says to his partner,
"I'm thinkin' of gettin' a cheese toastie.
Want one?"

His partner says,
"Absolutely not!
But if you're getting one,
can you have them cut it in half?
Just in case."

She grins.

❖ ❖ ❖

❖ ❖ ❖

A man (80s?)
wearing an Indiana Jones-style fedora,
greets a friend by calling out,
"Found 'em!"
and holds two cheese scones
in the air
like they're precious artifacts
raided from an ancient,
flour dusted temple.

❖ ❖ ❖

❖ ❖ ❖

A young human (10?)
runs through the markets roaring,
"MUM! MUM! MUM!
DAD JUST BOUGHT YOU A PONCHO!"

Mum masks a smile
and clutches her chest dramatically,
saying,
"A poncho?!"

Young Human Broadcasting System
nods emphatically.
"A Poncho!
Can you
BELIEVE IT?"

❖ ❖ ❖

❖ ❖ ❖

A very big dog
has found a stick in a park.

Not just any stick!
A stick that must definitely be thrown!

He bounds up to a woman (80s?)
with a walker,
and drops it,
looking at her expectantly.

She tells him she can't reach it,
and he politely picks it up
so she can throw it.

It doesn't go far,
but he gives her a mighty tail wag
for effort.

❖ ❖ ❖

❖ ❖ ❖

A small human (4?)
is belting along on her scooter
but she's just not happy with her speed.

There has to be something
that'll help her go faster...
something...

Hmm.

She scrunches up her face really tightly
and yes...

This FEELS faster.
Yes, definitely much faster.
She tells Dad as much.

Sometimes perception is
EVERYTHING.

❖ ❖ ❖

❖ ❖ ❖

Two birdlike women (80s?)
wearing brightly coloured
knitted berets and cardigans,
are meandering through the markets.

They're snuggled up together,
arm in arm
with their heads bowed
as one chuckles conspiratorially
at something the other one's just said.

❖ ❖ ❖

A young human (7?)
is getting overwhelmed
by all the lunchtime choices on offer.

Dad crouches next to him and says,
"Take a breath bud.
Okay. Another one.
Want a hug?"

Young Human nods yes
and visibly relaxes.

A few moments later he's seen
happily munching a hot dog.

❖ ❖ ❖

A small human (4?)
runs up to a big man
wearing a Harley-Davidson T-shirt
and says,
"Uncle Josh! Wanna see my skills?!"

Uncle Josh nods seriously.
"Yeah. Most definitely."

A very complex and impressive display
of interpretive dance
and martial arts moves ensues.

The game face is everything.

❖ ❖ ❖

❖ ❖ ❖

A tiny human (2?)
is running up to nearby people and roaring,
"SEE YOU LATER ALIGATOR!"
before waiting expectantly.

Almost everyone gets it right and retorts,
"In a while crocodile,"
only to be rewarded with rapturous giggles.

❖ ❖ ❖

A tiny human (2?)
with tiny pigtails,
is doing a vigorous wobble dance
as she stands in front of
a violin-playing busker.

Violin Busker is playing a sad song
full of minor notes
but Tiny Dancer is having none of it.

Her expression is fiercely intense.

She's going to do a happy dance to this music
and that's final!

Spring

Spring in New Zealand is opening the windows and hearing sheep and lambs bleating on the nearby hills. It's snow melt, new leaves, flowers and bees buzzing around the garden. It's longer days and the first cicadas making a tentative chirping appearance. It's the first barbeque outside again. It's walking in the sunshine eating a buttery croissant or a delicious samosa while running into people who were away for the winter. It's the return of T-shirt weather with a jumper in your bag just in case. It's flowering jasmine, wafting down laneways, driveways and streets.

In spring, Aotearoa comes alive.

❖ ❖ ❖

A small human (3?)
is marching behind his family,
swinging the bag of spinach
he's been given to carry
around his head
like it's the world's healthiest morning star.

Doing his best fierce face.

❖ ❖ ❖

❖ ❖ ❖

A busker is juggling two balls
one-handedly
to the delight of a small human,
while holding his guitar
in the other.

Small Human looks at her dad
and asks loudly,
"HOW DOES HE DO THAT?"

Juggling Busker replies,
"Superpowers and panic."

❖ ❖ ❖

❖ ❖ ❖

A woman (60s?)
rolls her wheelchair up
to the display counter
of a cheese truck.

Winking to the small humans at her side,
she snaffles cheese samples for them
while out of the eyeline of the servers.

Small Human giggles
are definitely
giving the game away.

❖ ❖ ❖

❖ ❖ ❖

A woman (50s?)
dressed stylishly
in a long cardigan and green sneakers,
is holding a hand-crafted knife
at a knife maker's stall.

She says,
"I like a weighty knife,"
and gives the stall owner a small smile.

❖ ❖ ❖

❖ ❖ ❖

A man (20s?)

stops in his tracks

in the middle of a flow of people,

eyes tearing up,

obviously overwhelmed.

A stall owner steps out from behind her table

and asks if he needs a hug.

He says yes.

❖ ❖ ❖

❖ ❖ ❖

A man (70s?)
in scuffed black Doc Martens
is kneeling next to a shy small human (3?)
wearing a cable knit cardigan.

He says,
"This is the market.
If you're scared,
Grandad can carry you on his shoulders.
Would you like that?"

Small Human nods.

❖ ❖ ❖

❖ ❖ ❖

A woman (30s?)
kneels down next to a small human (5?)
in front of a sausage truck.

She says,
"Why don't we compromise?
We can buy some sausages
and cook them at home
so it's cheaper."

Small Human looks at her
for a long moment
before thrusting his hands out dramatically,
asking,
"But will it be an EXPERIENCE?!"

❖ ❖ ❖

❖ ❖ ❖

Two women approach a plant stall.

The older (80s?)
is wearing a pretty floral dress.
The younger (50s?)
is dressed in sensible jeans and a hoodie.

The younger says to the older,
"If you try and steal a cutting Mum,
I'll be so cross with you."

Mum laughs wickedly.

❖ ❖ ❖

❖ ❖ ❖

A woman (80s?)
wearing a bright green beanie
is smiling to herself
as she rides a mobility scooter
with a single tomato plant
in the front basket.

There's a faint breeze
which makes the plant wave
at the people she passes.

❖ ❖ ❖

❖ ❖ ❖

The drummer in a bagpipe band
is wiping away tears
from behind her sunglasses
after taking part in a rousing performance
in front of an appreciative crowd.

❖ ❖ ❖

❖ ❖ ❖

Two people (20s?)
are on a first date.

They're completely absorbed
in each other's company.

He's speaking fluent French.
She's replying in broken French,
her expression earnest.

His encouraging grin is infectious.

❖ ❖ ❖

❖ ❖ ❖

Two portly men (60s?)
are cheerfully walking along, chatting.

1st: "I could do with a snack. I'm fading away."

2nd: "Yeah. You're disappearing before my eyes."

1st: "Gonna turn into thin air at this rate.
It's a medical emergency mate."

They laugh and then line up
in front of a food truck.

❖ ❖ ❖

❖ ❖ ❖

A woman (70s?)
picks up a large cucumber
at a fruit and vegetable stall.

She sighs dramatically
as she holds it up
before grinning wickedly
at her friend.

Her friend shakes her head and says,
"Can't take you anywhere."

❖ ❖ ❖

✧ ✧ ✧

A woman (60s?)
in a blue and white shirt,
is vibing out to buskers.

Dancing with big swishy movements
through the onlooking crowd,
toes sometimes en pointe,
eyes closed.

✧ ✧ ✧

❖ ❖ ❖

Numerous people are sitting
in front of a cafe
that's situated in a lane.

Eyes closed,
faces pointed to a sunny blue sky
as they enjoy the day.

❖ ❖ ❖

❖ ❖ ❖

Possibly the world's most introverted busker
is softly playing what sounds like
an Elliott Smith song.

He's singing so quietly
it's almost impossible to hear him.

The vibe is incredibly gentle.
Money clinks into his guitar case.

❖ ❖ ❖

❖ ❖ ❖

Two men (50s?)

are ambling

with colourful cloth bags

full of fruit and vegetables.

One wraps his arm

around his partner's waist

and says,

"Do you have any spare change Darl?

I've gotta get some of those peonies

for the house."

❖ ❖ ❖

❖ ❖ ❖

A tall and burly Italian man (80s?)
with a wild head of silver hair,
approaches a smoked cheese stall.

He greets the small human
minding the counter with her dad
with a booming,
"Ciao bambina!"
spreading his arms wide, grinning.

❖ ❖ ❖

❖ ❖ ❖

A disgruntled man (60s?)
is sighing and saying to his wife,
"You don't have any room in your suitcase."

She glances up from the pottery
she was just admiring
and gives him a long look over her glasses.
"I will MAKE room if I WANT to."

She picks up a mug
with a magnificently determined expression.

❖ ❖ ❖

❖ ❖ ❖

A small human (3?)
is trying to convince
a very large dog
to eat a small twig covered in leaves.

Small Human looks optimistic.

Large Dog is looking speculatively
at nearby pastry stall.

❖ ❖ ❖

❖ ❖ ❖

A small human (4?)
wearing purple butterfly gumboots
is confidently strafing packed tables
in a busy cafe,
making sure people notice
the way her shoes light up
with each step.

Expression catwalk intense.

❖ ❖ ❖

❖ ❖ ❖

A cheerful woman (20s?)
with an infectiously bubbly laugh
is selling zines.

She tells a browsing woman
that the one she's looking at
is a deliciously tragic lesbian love story.

The browser grins,
"Sounds perfect."

❖ ❖ ❖

❖ ❖ ❖

A regal looking woman (80s?)
wearing a neon blue T-shirt
and a chunky matching necklace,
is making her way through a cafe
using a walker.

She approaches a table of women
of differing ages
and says,
"Park my chariot will you, Darl?"
to the nearest,
who places the walker by the wall.

❖ ❖ ❖

❖ ❖ ❖

A woman (30s?)
pauses in talking to a friend.

She turns to her son (4?)
saying,
"Get your hands out of your pants, bud."

Small Human is indignant.
"Why?"

"Because it's not something we do in public."

He looks at her
with an expression older than time.
"But it's warm!"

Mum's friend laughs.
"He's got a point!"

❖ ❖ ❖

❖ ❖ ❖

A man approaches a bakery truck and muses,
"I think I'll just stop and get a donut."

His partner laughs.
"Didn't you just have breakfast?"

He nods.
"Yeah, but first breakfast is just practice.
This is SECOND breakfast."

❖ ❖ ❖

❖ ❖ ❖

A young human (10?)
with a hank of hair over his eyes
is participating in a haka.

He's a head shorter than the other kids
but he makes up for it
in sheer fierceness.

The determination is everything.

❖ ❖ ❖

❖ ❖ ❖

At a Mask Carnivale:

A small human (5?)

is explaining to another small human

dressed as a dragon

that she is dressed as,

"A UNICORN!

AND A PRINCESS!

AND THE PRINCE WHO RESCUES

THE UNICORN!"

Her vehemence is very convincing.

❖ ❖ ❖

❖ ❖ ❖

At a Mask Carnivale:
A small human in a traditional
Chinese lion dance costume
is going solo lion
and is loving it.

Next to her,
another small human
is being a very shy lion
who seems much more focussed
on day dreaming
and smiling
at the onlooking crowd.

❖ ❖ ❖

✦ ✦ ✦

A woman (70s?)
in a bright yellow T-shirt
passes a stand selling
mushroom grow bags.

She says to her friend with a wicked grin,
"I asked about getting one of those
and they said the mushrooms
grow out of any hole."

Her friend snorts. "Any hole eh?"

She nods. "Any hole."

They burst into deliciously filthy cackles.

✦ ✦ ✦

✦ ✦ ✦

A woman (60?)
sits at an outdoor table
overlooking a bustling market crowd.

She takes a tube of rose-scented hand cream
out of her bag
and has just popped some on her hands
when her husband says,
"I like the smell of that. Can I have some too?"

She gives it to him with a smile.

✦ ✦ ✦

❖ ❖ ❖

A man (80s?)
protectively shepherds his wife
across a busy road
as she navigates it
with her walking frame.

She arrives at the other side
and kisses him on the cheek in thanks.

❖ ❖ ❖

❖ ❖ ❖

A woman (40s?)
running a natural remedy stall,
tells a customer
that she lives in the bush out of town
and seems delighted
when she learns the customer is
a country person too.

She asks,
"Where's your bush?"
and they begin excitedly
talking local herbs.

❖ ❖ ❖

❖ ❖ ❖

A young human (8?)
is piggy backing a tiny human (2?)
who is wearing a sparkly tutu
and some star-shaped sunglasses.

Tiny Human is very wiggly
and heavy
and is dictatorially
roaring instructions.

Young Human
perseveres magnificently.

❖ ❖ ❖

❖ ❖ ❖

A small human (6?)
is the fairest fairy in all the land.

She's wearing flower garlands,
face paint,
a tutu
and bare feet
with coke-bottle-lens glasses.

She brandishes a wooden sword
at distant mountains
and roars.

❖ ❖ ❖

❖ ❖ ❖

Multiple small humans
are sliding down an invitingly steep grassy hill.

One is equipped with a cardboard box
and triumphantly scoots to the bottom.

The others are making do
with the seats of their pants.

Friction is winning
but they persevere valiantly.

❖ ❖ ❖

✦ ✦ ✦

A woman (30s?)
sitting on a hay bale,
is mediating a very complex
peace treaty
between two small humans.

It seems one took off
with the other's bowl of potatoes
and ate all the ones with
tomato sauce on them.

Tomato-sauce-covered fingers
are being pointed
and tissues
are being dispensed liberally.

✦ ✦ ✦

At a Country Spring Fair:
A young human (7?)
is strutting
to a pony riding
and marshmallow toasting glen.

His swagger is epic.

He's got bare feet
and is nonchalantly
munching a sandwich.

His little brother (4?)
is trotting along behind him,
copying his every movement.

Hero worship is a very real thing.

✦ ✦ ✦

At an Agricultural Show:
A small human at the top of a Ferris wheel
roars,
"MUUUM I REALLY NEED TO WEE!"
down to their mum waiting below.

The suspense
for the rest of the ride
is intense.

✦ ✦ ✦

At an Agricultural Show:
A tiny human (2?)
is looking in awe at a fire truck
with open doors.

A fireman offers to give him a tour of the inside
and Tiny Human looks at Dad
in wide-eyed disbelief.

This much greatness
can't exist in the world,
surely?

❖ ❖ ❖

At an Agricultural Show:
A teen is patting a rotund donkey's ears.

She's smiling to herself.
This is exactly where she wants to be.

Meanwhile, Donkey is intent on snuffling
Teen's pockets for any hidden hay bales
or giant bags of oats
she may have concealed
on her person.

Just in case.

❖ ❖ ❖

❖ ❖ ❖

At an Agricultural Show:
A chill young human (9?)
is riding her very opinionated Arabian pony
in an equestrian event.

Other young humans
are trotting sedately
in a circle before a judge.

But Opinionated Pony
has places to go
and things to see
and they're on
the other side of the field.

❖ ❖ ❖

❖ ❖ ❖

At an Agricultural Show:
A tractor stand has been set up
across from a crystal display.

A man (40s?)
nudges a friend
and says with a smirk,
"Do you believe in
the healing power of crystals, mate?"

The friend shakes his head
and says pensively,
"Nah mate. Nah. But I DO believe
in the healing power of tractors eh."

❖ ❖ ❖

❖ ❖ ❖

At an Agricultural Show:
A tiny human (2?)
in tiny work boots
and no-nonsense shorts
is standing eye to eye
with a very woolly lamb.

Both Tiny Human and Tiny Sheep
are regarding each other warily.

They are not quite sure
what all this fuss is about.

❖ ❖ ❖

❖ ❖ ❖

A no-nonsense woman
is in line at a pâtisserie stand.

She buys pastries,
then, unprompted, abruptly says,
"I have a food philosophy.
This is a part of it.
It's not a joke."

The pâtissier shrugs with Gallic chill.
"Pastries are serious.
I don't question people's choices."

❖ ❖ ❖

❖ ❖ ❖

A woman (50s?)
passes a Māori fried bread truck.

She grins and exclaims,
"We've GOT to get some
for the whānau."

She immediately orders eight.

Her husband tries to correct her by saying,
"How about we get two?
They're pretty big."

He immediately gets
THE LOOK
and hurriedly says,
"Yeah, eight is about right."

❖ ❖ ❖

❖ ❖ ❖

Two men (20s?)
meet in front of a pizza stall.

1st: "How ya goin' mate. Alright. Yeah?"
2nd: "Yeah… Alright… Yeah. You alright?"
1st: "Yeah mate. Alright. Yeah"
2nd: "Alright"
1st: "Yeah"

Profundity achieved,
they go on their way,
smiling.

❖ ❖ ❖

❖ ❖ ❖

A man (70s?)

with his face and arms covered in tattoos,

is pushing a tiny human in a pram.

Grandad is making car noises

as they're going along

and this is a V8 supercharged vehicle.

Tiny Human's chortles of happiness

turn into outright cackles

when they screech around a corner.

❖ ❖ ❖

❖ ❖ ❖

A woman (20s?)
wearing muddy hiking boots
and weighed down
with a battered looking backpack,
weaves through a crowd.

She's holding a bouquet of lavender
to her nose,
inhaling deeply as she goes.

❖ ❖ ❖

A small human (3?)
watches on
as his dad and two French tourists
talk local attractions.

Small Human frowns.
Small Human fidgets.

Finally he makes his move and roars,
"I HAVE TWO GUINEA PIGS!"

This vital information imparted,
he awaits their awe.

❖ ❖ ❖

A tiny human (2?)
wearing a strawberry hat,
sits on her dad's shoulders
as he orders at a coffee cart.

Tiny Strawberry cares not for coffee.

She regards her surroundings
from her great height
with an imperiousness
that befits her elevated status.

❖ ❖ ❖

The Year's End & Christmas

Christmas time in New Zealand is browsing for delicious things to eat on sunny days. It's looking for gifts and enjoying seeing other people doing their shopping. It's festive barbeques and bare feet in the garden. It's going to Christmas fairs to buy homemade fruit cakes. It's time spent with friends in beer gardens that smell of jasmine and greenery. It's tinsel on pushbikes and Christmas T-shirts. It's a time for thinking of others close and far away. It's people laughing and enjoying each other's company. It's making time for friends who are finding the festive season difficult. It's a time for reflection and relaxation.

Christmas in Aotearoa is togetherness.

❖ ❖ ❖

A small human (4?)
in a stripy dress
is solemnly attempting to pay for a toy
with a half-eaten apple.

Her expression becomes incensed
when she discovers that apples,
even precious half-eaten ones,
aren't legal tender.

❖ ❖ ❖

✦ ✦ ✦

A woman (60s?)
in a flowing floral shirt
scoops her newborn granddaughter from a pram,
hugs her close
and inhales deeply.

She sighs and smiles at her daughter.

"There's something about the way
a baby's head smells.
Magical!"

Tiny New Human doesn't seem to mind.
She's fast asleep.

✦ ✦ ✦

❖ ❖ ❖

A small human (4?)
snaffles a baguette
that's been stored in the bottom
of his sister's pram.

Raising it in the air
like a mighty bread blade,
he bellows a war cry
and bolts through the crowd.

He's a tiny warrior off to battle,
with his laughing dad in hot pursuit.

❖ ❖ ❖

❖ ❖ ❖

A man (20s?)
in a preppy outfit and boat shoes
stands on tiptoes to straighten the collar
of his much taller boyfriend's shirt.

His boyfriend grins
and steals a kiss
before telling him to stop fussing.

❖ ❖ ❖

❖ ❖ ❖

A young human (9?)
is listening to a busker
play a rather good acoustic version
of Dolly Parton's *Jolene*.

She asks her mum,
"Hey Mum.
Do you know what this song is about?"

Her mum doesn't skip a beat when she answers,
"Your aunt."

❖ ❖ ❖

❖ ❖ ❖

A woman (40s?)
leans against a tree
while talking to a man (70s?)

She says,
"I worked in emergency rooms for twenty years
before I moved here for the slower pace."

He nods.
"Right decision?"

She smiles.
"Yeah. Right decision."

❖ ❖ ❖

❖ ❖ ❖

A small human (5?)
is determinedly running point-to-point
between stalls on a grassy field.

Only he knows why,
but he is doing it with purpose
and commitment
like a pint-sized
display of Brownian motion
in sandals and a bucket hat.

❖ ❖ ❖

❖ ❖ ❖

A woman (30s?)
is looking down at a small human (3?)
dressed as a VERY dishevelled fairy.
"Kayla, where is your shoe?"

Small Human glances at her
unshod foot,
looks up and grins.
"I'm selling it for Christmas!"

A determined search
of all market stalls
for a small human's shoe commences.

❖ ❖ ❖

❖ ❖ ❖

A couple (80s?)
are sitting at an outside cafe table
reading paperbacks.

She looks up and asks,
"Do you love me?"

He answers,
"Profoundly. Why do you ask?"

She shrugs with a small smile.
"Just checking."

They go back to reading.

❖ ❖ ❖

A very sneaky Golden Retriever
has managed to get her head
into her human's shopping bag
while her human is talking to friends.

Sneaky Dog mistakenly chomps
on some spring onions and sneezes,
giving the game away.

These were not the delicious treats
she was looking for!

❖ ❖ ❖

A small human (4?)
in a floral dress
is clutching a sparkly purse to her chest
as she is comforted by her dad.

Looking out at the crowd before her
with a quivering lip
she wails,
"But I don't WANT
to buy anyone
Christmas presents!"

❖ ❖ ❖

A small human (3?)
in a green hat
is told by his mum not to run ahead
as they navigate a busy crowd.

He turns and huffs
a long-suffering sigh.
"But I'm showing you the way
so you don't get lost!"

❖ ❖ ❖

A very big man

with sleeve tattoos and a shaved head

is sitting on a bench

with his very big staffy

keeping him company.

Big Man and Big Dog

are resting their heads against each other.

Both human and dog are smiling

in happiness.

This is real love.

❖ ❖ ❖

❖ ❖ ❖

A man (30s?)
is standing in a long line
for barbeque pork rolls
while patiently undoing
a tangle of braids
that his small human (6?)
has done in her hair,
then redoing them.

The air smells delicious,
the vibe is chill.

❖ ❖ ❖

❖ ❖ ❖

A small human (5?)
in Christmas board shorts and a Hulk T-shirt
hefts a magnificent watermelon.

Mum asks if it's too heavy
but Christmas Hulk knows not heavy!

Christmas Hulk can lift,
"Millions of these!"

❖ ❖ ❖

❖ ❖ ❖

A man (30s?)
orders five pieces of fried chicken
at a food truck.

His partner raises a brow.
"You alright there?
We're gonna be eating tons this afternoon."

He nods grinning.
"Yeah. With the aunties. I gotta prepare myself."

They both walk off,
munching Auntie Fortification Chicken
as they go.

❖ ❖ ❖

❖ ❖ ❖

A woman (50s?)
in a linen dress,
hugs a friend.

Linen Dress asks,
"You looking forward to a
family Christmas this year?"

Her friend hoots with laughter.
"Hell no!
I see them every day!
Why'd I want to see them at Christmas?
I talked them into going to Bali for a holiday!"

They share a huge conspiratorial grin.

❖ ❖ ❖

And here we reach the end of this book.

Thank you so much
for roaming through these pages,
and wherever you are in the world,
whatever your situation,
I hope you find your own
tiny moments of joy.

Glossary of Common Words, Phrases and Days

Aotearoa: Is the Māori name for New Zealand.
Aroha: To love, to feel compassion or empathy.
Chilly Bin: A cooler, or an Esky if you're Aussie.
Dairy: A corner shop. (Or your local equivalent.)
Feijoa: A green fruit that's iconically Kiwi. (Even thought they originated in South America.) Almost every house in my street has one or multiple feijoa trees.
Fluffies: Are frothed hot milk with a topping of choice. Sometimes called babyccinos in other parts of the world.
Footpath: Sidewalk or pavement.
Freedom Camping: Is camping on a site with no facilities with the expectation that you'll leave the site as you found it. It's very common in Aotearoa New Zealand, especially in the summer time.
Gumboots: Wellies or rubber boots.
Jandals: Flip flops, or thongs.
Jumper: A sweater.
Kapa Haka: The name for Māori action songs and the groups that perform them.
Kiwi: A person from Aotearoa New Zealand. A flightless bird who lays extraordinarily large eggs for its size. Also a delicious fruit.
Kōwhai: A native New Zealand tree with brilliant

yellow flowers.

Lollies: Sweets or candy.

Māori Fried Bread (Parāoa Parai): Carbohydrate deliciousness. Think savoury donuts.

Marae: A communal or sacred place that serves religious and social purposes.

Matariki: Māori New Year. It's a celebration of the first rising of Matariki (the Pleiades star cluster) in late June or early July.

Op Shop: A shortening of 'opportunity shop'. A thrift store or charity shop.

Pies: Pies in Aotearoa come in multiple forms, but the term 'pie' refers to a small single-serve savoury pie, often eaten on the go. If it's a sweet pie or a slice of pie, that will be mentioned.

Poffertjes: Tiny, fluffy Dutch pancakes. Often sprinkled with icing sugar.

Rug Up: To keep warm.

Sausage in a bun and hot dogs: When you see the term 'sausage in a bun', I'm referring to German-style wurst served in a small bun. When you see hot dog, I'm referring to the American style hot dog with a longer bun and an American style sausage.

Singlet: A tank top or vest.

To Shout: To buy. Used exclusively in situations when

you're buying someone something. You can shout your friends a round of drinks. Or shout your sister dinner.

Small Human: Anyone ranging roughly from 2 to 6 years old. (My term.)

Sweet As: Means awesome, great, fantastic.

Tiny Human: Anyone raging roughly from newborn to 2 years old. (My term.)

Tomato Sauce: Tomato ketchup.

Ute: A utility vehicle. Think a smaller version of an American-style truck.

Waiata: A song/songs.

Waitangi Day: The national day of Aotearoa New Zealand. It marks the anniversary of the initial signing of the Treaty of Waitangi on 6 February 1840.

Whānau: Family and extended family.

Young Human: Anyone ranging roughly from 6 to 12 years old. (My term.)

Wharenui: An ancestral meeting house.

Please Note: New Zealand embraces many immigrant communities and their holidays and special days are celebrated throughout the year as well.

Special Thanks

An extra special and heartfelt thanks goes to:

    Rachel Clifton
    Aaron Soto
    Joseph Brown
    Lillian Whitmore
    Leanna Dobson

You guys are simply amazing and I'm so incredibly grateful to you for your positivity, kindness and wonderful support.

Acknowledgements

I'm incredibly grateful to my wonderful Patreon and Buy Me a Coffee supporters. Thank you so much!

I'd also like to thank my lovely partner Tony Johnson, who was with me on almost all of these forays to markets and fairs and frequently spotted things before I did!

The way a person views a place is inevitably shaped by the friends they make when they first arrive. And here, I owe a world of gratitude to the wonderful people of Whakatū Nelson, Tasman and Golden Bay who've made us feel so welcome these past two years. Thank you!

About The Author

George Penney is a best-selling comedy fiction author who has lived a determinedly eccentric life. She spends her spare time people watching, voraciously reading and embracing her new home in Aotearoa New Zealand with her partner in crime and frequent co-author, Tony Johnson.

For all book links, social media links and other shenanigans you can visit:

www.swashbucklerpress.com

Also By The Author

Non Fiction

More Tiny Moments of Joy (Coming Soon)

Cosy Fantasy Mystery
(with Tony Johnson)

OverLondon

Rude Mechanicals (Coming Soon)

Fiction Written As Evie Snow

Fly In Fly Out

Love Imperfection

The Barbershop Girl

Save Me From Heroes

Ian Buchanan's Very Big Secret

This is Not a F*cking Romance

The Trouble With Darcy

The Beard

Mind Games

Stuck on You

Sweet on You

Head Over Heels

❖ ❖ ❖

Any typos spotted in this book are a variety of Profanity Inducing Little Sausage who delight in thwarting authors and copy, line and proof editors with glee. If spotted, please compliment them on their sneakiness and maybe let them roam free. If they've managed to survive this long, they're probably meant to be here as a reminder that humans aren't perfect and it's the imperfections that make us wonderful.

www.ingramcontent.com/pod-product-compliance
Lightning Source LLC
Chambersburg PA
CBHW022215090526
44584CB00012BB/554